RAINBOW ALLIES

THE TRUE STORY OF KIDS WHO STOOD AGAINST HATE

NANCY
CHURNIN

ILLUSTRATED BY
IZZY EVANS

beaming books
MINNEAPOLIS

Published in 2024 by Beaming Books, an imprint of 1517 Media. All rights reserved.
No part of this book may be reproduced without the written permission of the publisher.
Email copyright@1517.media.

30 29 28 27 26 25 24   1 2 3 4 5 6 7 8 9

Library of Congress Cataloging-in-Publication Data

Names: Churnin, Nancy, author. | Evans, Izzy, illustrator.
Title: Rainbow allies : the true story of kids who stood against hate / by
   Nancy Churnin ; illustrated by Izzy Evans.
Description: Minneapolis : Beaming Books, 2024. | Audience: Ages 5–8 |
   Summary: "The true story of how a Massachusetts neighborhood rallied
   together to help a lesbian couple feel welcome and loved again after
   experiencing anti-LGBTQ hate"– Provided by publisher.
Identifiers: LCCN 2023023126 (print) | LCCN 2023023127 (ebook) | ISBN
   9781506488448 (hardback) | ISBN 9781506488455 (ebook)
Subjects: LCSH: Lesbian couples–Massachusetts–Juvenile literature. |
   Allyship–Massachusetts–Juvenile literature. |
   Homophobia–Massachusetts–Juvenile literature.
Classification: LCC HQ76.26 .C48 2024 (print) | LCC HQ76.26 (ebook) | DDC
   306.76–dc23/eng/20231010
LC record available at https://lccn.loc.gov/2023023126
LC ebook record available at https://lccn.loc.gov/2023023127

Hardcover ISBN: 978-1-5064-8844-8
eBook ISBN: 978-1-5064-8845-5

Beaming Books
PO Box 1209
Minneapolis, MN 55440-1209
Beamingbooks.com

Printed in China.

For Cari and Lauri Ryding and their community for trusting me with their story and for wonderful couples that I love, including dear friends and family Nancy and Sarah, Patricia and Rebecca, Dory and Sabby, Roger and Brett. Proud to be an ally. —**NC**

For Ma and Pa, who love me unconditionally. —**IE**

In Natick, Massachusetts, there is a neighborhood that looks like many others. It isn't the biggest or the fanciest. Many pass through, not realizing the secret that makes it shine: everyone is welcome; everyone is celebrated; everyone helps each other. Kids play at each other's houses, dogs greet one another on walks, and adults buy lemonade from the children's stands.

When people move in, neighbors bring a bounty of foods from their different cultures so they can enjoy the many flavors of their new home.

When Cari, one of the neighbors, married, everyone was happy to meet her wife, Lauri. Their dogs, Twink and Scout, were welcomed too.

"We've got something for you!" Brendan, one of the neighborhood kids, said, pulling dog biscuits from a bowl. Twink and Scout smothered Brendan, Landon, and Sommer with kisses. They wagged tails as they crunched treats. "Twink and Scout say thank you," Cari said as she bought lemonade.

Landon saw a bright cloth peeking out of Lauri's bag.

"What's that?" he asked.

"It's a rainbow flag," Lauri said, pulling it out to show them. "Do you think it will look nice on our house?"

"It's beautiful!" Sommer said, her fingers tracing the bright colors.

"Can we help put it up?" Brendan asked. Landon nodded eagerly.

"We have a ladder," Sommer said.

Cari and Lauri loved their neighborhood where everyone was welcome.

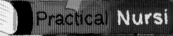

Then one day, when Brendan passed their house, something felt wrong. He squeezed his brakes. It was too quiet—no Twink or Scout scampering to greet him. He didn't even hear a bark.

And something else was missing. Was it...their flag?

Brendan saw Cari and Lauri scrubbing sticky bits of yolk from their walls and windows. Twink and Scout were whimpering, curled in balls by their feet. A broken mount swayed where the flag had waved.

"What happened?" Brendan whispered.

Cari told him they'd found the house this way when they got home.
"Why?" Brendan felt the hurt his friends were feeling like a stone in his
stomach. Nothing like this had ever happened in his neighborhood before.

"Maybe someone doesn't like our flag," Lauri said.
"Maybe someone doesn't like *us*," Cari added.

"Can you get another flag?" Brendan asked.

"And have someone do this again?" Lauri wiped her eyes. "I'm sorry, Brendan. I thought this was a neighborhood where everyone is welcome. But now?"

That was what Brendan loved about his neighborhood too—that everyone was welcome! Had it changed? Was it broken, like Cari and Lauri's flag? How could it be fixed? How could Cari and Lauri feel welcome again?

Brendan pedaled slowly to the lemonade stand.
He told his friends what happened.

Sommer kicked a rock.

"Why would anyone do that?" she asked.

They thought and thought. None of them had an answer. So they thought of another question . . .

"What can we do?" Sommer said at last.

"I've seen rainbow flags at a store," Landon said. "Can we get them another one?"

Brendan sighed. "Lauri is worried that someone might steal it or egg their house again."

Sommer lined up some paper cups and pushed them close together.

"What if we built a wall around their house?"

Brendan scratched his head. "Or we could set up a patrol and take turns guarding their porch?"

Landon clenched his fist.
"Or we could find out who did this and egg their house too."

But none of their ideas seemed right for a neighborhood where everyone was welcome. They didn't want to separate their friends with a wall, or treat others like enemies. They needed to find a way to bring everyone together, to show love that was big enough to heal the hurt.

Then, suddenly, a plan came to them. But would it work?

Could they get other kids to help?
Would their neighbors come through?

Brendan, Landon, and Sommer biked to the store that had the flags. They told the man at the counter what they wanted to do. He grinned.

"Take as many as you want," he said. He helped load them on their bikes.

As they rolled by, kids playing in the street asked what they were doing with the flags.

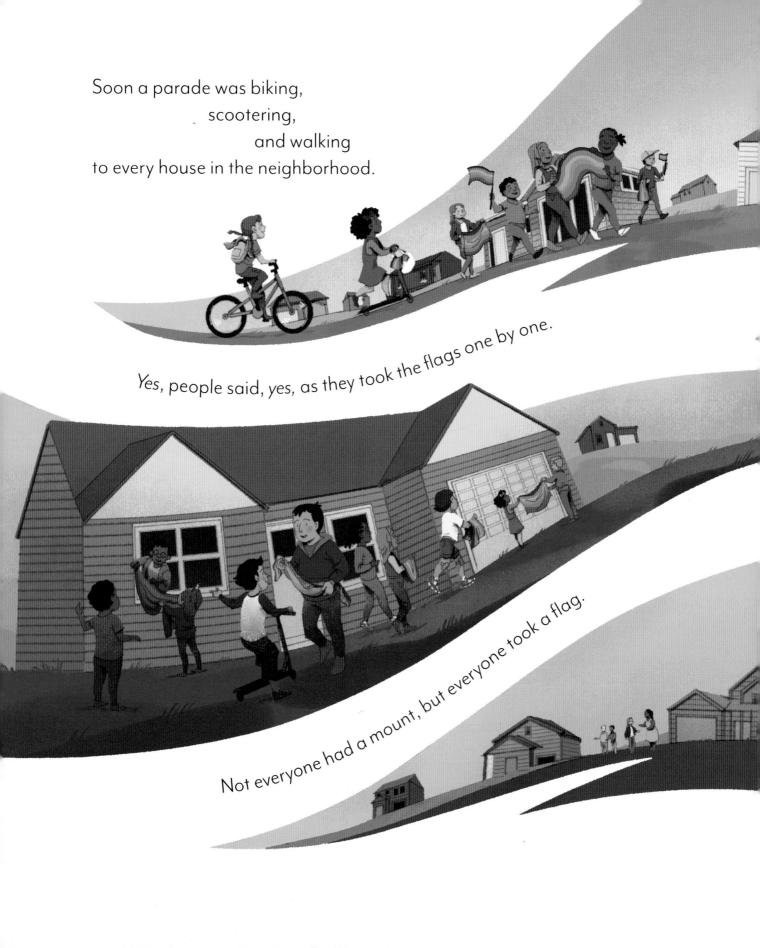

Soon a parade was biking,
scootering,
and walking
to every house in the neighborhood.

Yes, people said, yes, as they took the flags one by one.

Not everyone had a mount, but everyone took a flag.

Some hung a flag on a door,

some across a porch,

some on a fence,

and one in a big tree!

The children brought the last flag to Cari and Lauri's house.
They cheered as Cari and Lauri hung the flag on their door. Twink and Scout jumped and slobbered on hands and faces.

Together Cari, Lauri, adults, and kids walked up and down the bumpy sidewalks.

Together they admired how all the families were different but united, like the different colors in the rainbows of the flags.

The children waved goodbye to Cari, to Lauri, to each other, to everyone, glowing with pride as they biked, scootered, and walked home. The kids had done it! They'd taken something broken and made it beautiful.

Once again, their neighborhood was a place where everyone is welcome.
Where everyone is celebrated. Where everyone helps each other.

AUTHOR'S NOTE

In August of 2016 a married couple, Cari and Lauri Ryding, returned to their home in Natick, Massachusetts, to find their rainbow flag stolen, their front porch pelted with eggs, and their dogs, Twink and Scout, so distressed that they had to take them to the vet, where Scout was hooked up to IVs.

Cari and Lauri had always felt so loved and accepted in their community, where neighbors attended their wedding on October 19, 2012. They wondered if they would ever feel that way again. Then friends found a way to show the couple their love. With the support of parents, the children—including Brendan and Landon and Sommer—went to the Rainbow Peace Flag Project, where Cari and Lauri had gotten their flag. They got enough flags for the whole neighborhood!

The act was in the spirit of the people of Billings, Montana, whose response in 1993 to a brick being thrown through the bedroom window of a five-year-old Jewish boy displaying a menorah was for thousands of citizens to paste pictures of menorahs in their windows.

And here was another extraordinary thing about the flags: their message of welcome, celebration, and kindness spread. When people from other neighborhoods saw the flags or read or heard what the children had done, they hung rainbow flags in their communities too.

I am thankful to Cari and Lauri and the families in their community for sharing their story about the difference a caring gesture can make.

"It's completely transformed the experience for us," Lauri told me. "We are very grateful to the children for standing with us and showing the world that kindness and love matter."

HOW TO BE AN LGBTQ ALLY

How did the families in Lauri and Cari's neighborhood raise their children to be allies? Lauri and Cari asked their neighbors for tips on raising kind kids. This is what the parents told them:

BE A GOOD FRIEND

When bad things happen, say, "These are our friends and they are hurting. They deserve to be happy. How can we make them feel better?"

DON'T TEACH HATE

Kids don't see any difference between same-sex and opposite-sex marriage. If you don't teach them differently, they remain open and welcoming of all families.

TAKE ACTION

Hurt feelings can fester. If a bully says something hurtful to someone in your presence, don't be a bystander—be an upstander and speak up. If a bully does something hurtful, like the person who egged the house and took away the rainbow flag, take quick action to show your friends that you love and support them.

RALLY OTHERS, BUT DON'T FORCE THEM

There is strength in numbers, but don't judge those who don't join you in taking action. Celebrate and focus on those who are willing to spread love and kindness.

NANCY CHURNIN is an award-winning children's book author who writes about people who have made the world a better place and who inspire children to be heroes too. Her titles include *Dear Mr. Dickens*; *A Queen to the Rescue: The Story of Henrietta Szold, Founder of Hadassah*; and *Irving Berlin: The Immigrant Boy Who Made America Sing*, among dozens of others. Her work has received numerous awards and honors including the National Jewish Book Award, the Sydney Taylor Honor, and Junior Library Guild selections.

Born and raised in New York City, Nancy lives in North Texas, where she enjoyed being a theater critic for *The Dallas Morning News* before becoming a full-time author.

IZZY EVANS is an illustrator, animator, and weekend flapjack baker from North London, England. Their work is best known for its diverse characters, gentle humor, and the occasional unicorn. Izzy draws inspiration from nature, mythology, and the multicultural history of their city to create their work. In the future, they aspire to have a studio in a little cottage in the country, where they can keep chickens, grow potatoes, and write stories.